Nature's Children

PET DOGS

by Frank Puccio

GROLIER
EDUCATIONAL

FACTS IN BRIEF

Classification of dogs.

Class:	*Mammalia* (mammals)
Order:	*Carnivora* (meat eaters)
Family:	*Canidae* (dogs, wolves, jackals, foxes)
Genus:	*Canis* (dogs)
Species:	*Canis familiaris* (the domestic dog)

World distribution. Native to all parts of the world except Australia, New Zealand, and other islands in the ocean. Dogs in those areas have been introduced by humans.

Habitat. Dogs have adapted to many habitats, including deserts, rain forests, and very cold climates.

Distinctive physical characteristics. Adapted for pursuing and capturing prey, most dogs have long legs and a narrow, elongated skull with sharp teeth.

Habits. In the wild dogs live in groups called packs, with one dominant leader. Domestic dogs transfer pack loyalty to their human owners and family.

Diet. Dogs are basically meat-eaters, but they can also eat cooked grains and vegetables. 132-8610

Library of Congress Cataloging-in Publication Data

Puccio, Frank, 1956-
  Pet Dogs / Frank Puccio.
    p.   cm. — (Nature's Children)
  Includes index.
  Summary: Describes the physical characteristics, behavior,
distribution, and care of various types of domestic dogs.
  ISBN 0-7172-9066-2 (hardbound)
  1. Dogs—Juvenile literature   [1. Dogs.]   I. Title.
II. Series.
SF426.5.P83   1997
636.7'0887—dc21

97-5970
CIP
AC

This library reinforced edition was published in 1997 exclusively by:

Grolier Educational

Sherman Turnpike, Danbury, Connecticut 06816

Set ISBN 0-7172-7661-9
Pet Dogs ISBN 0-7172-9066-2

Contents

Have you ever heard the phrase "man's best friend"? If you have, you probably know that it describes a dog. Dogs have lived with humans for thousands of years, helping them, protecting them, and working for them. And they have been family pets for thousands of years too, giving people love, comfort, and companionship.

Today there are hundreds of kinds of dogs, with a dog to suit just about every kind of person. Do you want a big dog or a little one? A mild-mannered dog or a fierce guard dog? Do you want a playful, active dog or one that will spend quiet hours with you as you sit and read or just relax? Choosing the right dog is a matter of knowing who you are and what you want—and finding a pet to match.

As you probably already know, dogs are a lot of fun. But they also are a lot of work. Dogs need care and companionship just as people do. But the hours of care you give will be rewarded with a lifetime of friendship and loyalty.

Dogs can be special friends to people of all ages.

Dogs and Humans: The Beginnings

Dogs are generally considered the first domesticated animals. Since the days of the Stone Age dogs have lived with humans. Cave paintings, statues, and tools from prehistoric times all show that dogs did everything from guard their masters to help hunters find and kill wild game. Civilizations, such as the Egyptians and the Greeks, came to depend on dogs for their keen hunting instincts, their ability to herd flocks of goats or sheep, and their willingness to defend and protect their masters.

Today some types of dogs are still used to herd and hunt. Other, specially trained dogs perform daring rescues, sniff out bombs or illegal drugs, and assist people with impaired vision or hearing. Dogs also perform in circuses, dog races, and organized shows and competitions.

For most of us, however, dogs are mainly for friendship and companionship. As the first dog owners discovered, regardless of the task a dog does, its main ties to its masters are those of love, loyalty, and devotion.

Dogs do many jobs for people, but most of all they provide love and friendship.

Dogs like this Boston terrier are the result of many years of careful breeding.

Where Did They Come From?

At first glance there seems to be little connection between the modern pet dog—from a tiny, slender dachshund to a large rottweiler—and the wolves and coyotes that still run wild today. But domestic dogs are most likely descended from wolves that lived many thousands of years ago.

Some scientists believe that some of these wolves may have hung around human camps to eat any food discarded by people. Very gradually the wolves that were least afraid of humans probably drifted into the camps. Eventually they became tame. Their relatives who avoided humans stayed wild. Humans probably helped in this selection process by killing or driving off the creatures that were unwilling to draw closer to people.

Humans probably started selecting and breeding their dogs for specific traits at an early time. Perhaps hunting skills appealed to some people, or a certain fur color was considered valuable or lucky. Perhaps a loud bark or a sweet nature was wanted. Whatever the choices and however long the changes took, today's domestic dogs, with their less powerful teeth and jaws, their upturned tails, and their tamer personalities are quite different from their wild relatives.

Dog Breeds

The American Kennel Club, the nonprofit organization that regulates dog shows in the United States, recognizes 140 pure breeds of dogs. Other countries have similar groups. In the United Kingdom, for example, the Kennel Club of England lists 210 dog breeds. Clearly there are many different kinds of dogs from which to choose!

The American Kennel Club classifies dogs in seven groups based on their appearance, function, and size. These groups include sporting dogs, hounds, working dogs, terriers, toy dogs, nonsporting dogs, and herding dogs. The different breeds—collies, golden retrievers, poodles, or whatever—fall into these seven categories.

These recognized breeds, however, are not all there is in the world of dogs. A dog might also be a mongrel, meaning that its parents are of different or mixed breeds. Some people even prefer mixed breeds—or mutts, as they sometimes are called. But regardless of how wonderful a pet a mixed breed is, it will not be recognized by any kennel club. These clubs only register purebred dogs, or dogs of traceable ancestry.

The American Kennel Club (the AKC) recognizes 140 different dog breeds—including the golden retriever like this young pup.

Sporting Dogs

Sporting dogs help hunters find and retrieve small game. Pointers, setters, retrievers, and spaniels are all breeds of sporting dogs.

Pointers and setters are trained to show hunters where animals are hiding. When they find prey, these dogs stand on point. Remaining as still as possible, these dogs stand with their noses pointed toward the game until the hunter is within range. Pointers include German shorthaired pointers, German wirehaired pointers, and the wire-haired pointing griffon. Setter breeds do much the same thing, although they originally were trained to sit, rather than point, when they saw game. Popular setters include English, Irish, and Gordon setters.

Retrievers fetch wounded or killed game. These dogs willingly charge across fields or jump into cold ponds or freezing ocean waters to collect the dead or injured game. Golden retrievers and Labrador retrievers are breeds of this type.

Spaniels flush, or chase, birds from their hiding places in bushes and tall grasses. Spaniel breeds include cocker spaniels, Brittany spaniels, and English springer spaniels.

Brittany spaniels are a popular pet dog that began as a hunting dog.

Hounds

Dogs in the hound group were developed to hunt. They are distinguished by a sharp sense of smell or sight, great physical stamina, and distinctive barking.

Basset hounds, bloodhounds, beagles, and foxhounds are examples of scent hounds. These breeds use their keen sense of smell to hunt. Bloodhounds have the best sniffing ability of all dog breeds. They can follow a trail of scent that is many days old.

Other hounds, known as gaze hounds or sight hounds, use their keen vision to find their prey. Basenjis, one of the oldest dog breeds, are sight hounds that can hunt, point, retrieve, or race. The first basenjis were given as gifts to the pharaohs of ancient Egypt. Basenjis are the only dogs that cannot bark. Instead, they communicate by making an unusual whining sound. Other sight hounds include greyhounds, salukis, and Afghan hounds.

Considered glamorous pets today, Afghan hounds began as hunters that used their keen eyesight to find game.

Terriers

The 25 recognized breeds of terriers were originally developed for their ability to dig into the earth to look for prey. Terriers are specialists in finding small animals like rabbits, weasels, groundhogs, and even rats.

Have you ever seen a miniature schnauzer? This breed of dog is a terrier as well, although no one today would dream of using one of these tiny dogs as a hunter. Miniature schnauzers have a wiry coat and can be gray, gray and black, or all black in color. Schnauzers make excellent family pets. They play well with children, are loyal to their families, and are good guard dogs.

Another terrier that makes a great pet is an Irish terrier. Known for its beautiful red coat, Irish terriers are good playmates and protect those they love. During World War I Irish terriers often were used as messenger dogs to carry documents and orders between army units.

Other terriers include bull terriers, fox terriers, Skye terriers, Manchester terriers, and Airedales, the largest terrier breed.

A miniature airedale terrier makes a cute and lovable pet.

Toy Dogs

Toy dogs are any of several breeds of very small dogs, all of whom are kept as pets. Some toy dogs, such as toy poodles and miniature pinschers, are smaller versions of large dog breeds. Others are breeds all their own. Regardless, however, within this group are some of the most unusual looking dogs of all.

The pug is the largest of the toy dogs and may weigh up to eighteen pounds (8.1 kilograms). It has a short muzzle (its nose and jaws) and a wrinkled face. Its unusual name probably came about in the early 1700s because it resembled another popular pet of that time, the marmoset monkey, which was called a "pug."

The Pekingese is sometimes called the "lion dog." The name might come from its appearance or perhaps from its independent and courageous spirit. It has a broad head, a short, flat, black nose, a short, wrinkled muzzle, heart-shaped ears, and a thick mane that forms a collar about the neck. Pekinese originally were bred in ancient China, where they were considered sacred.

Among the many other toy breeds are Chihuahuas, Maltese, Italian greyhounds, and Yorkshire terriers.

Working Dogs

Working dogs vary both in size and function. Some working dogs, like collies, German shepherds, or corgis, herd and protect animals. Others—rottweilers and Doberman pinschers, for example—guard homes and property. Still others, like huskies, pull sleds or carry packs.

Great Danes are the tallest of the working dogs. Males measure at least 30 inches (76 centimeters) high at the shoulders; females, 28 inches (71 centimeters). With their large, narrow heads and muscular bodies, Great Danes are an impressive sight.

Also impressive are two other working dogs that are used today primarily as guard dogs. These are the rottweiler and Doberman pinscher. Both are strong, fierce, and trustworthy. Boxers, Saint Bernards, Newfoundlands, and giant or standard schnauzers are among other popular breeds of working dogs.

Working dogs are usually courageous, alert, intelligent, loyal, and affectionate. Remarkably, these qualities also make working dogs excellent pets!

Nonsporting Dogs

If you are looking for a good companion dog, then one of the nonsporting dog breeds may be for you. Some of these were first developed for work or sport, but today they are mostly companion dogs or show dogs.

The poodle is one of the best-known breeds of nonsporting dog. First developed in France for duck hunting, poodles are now often the "show stoppers" at dog shows. They come in different sizes—toy (grouped with the toy breeds), miniature, and standard. Typically their curly coats are shaped, or clipped.

The bulldog, which comes from a long line of fighters, almost disappeared when dogfighting was outlawed in most European countries. Fans of the breed saved it. But the bulldogs they now breed are less ferocious than their ancestors. Still, the word bulldog continues to be used to describe a rough and tough fighter.

The pitbull is a crossbreed of a bulldog and a terrier. It is an especially aggressive animal with jaws that are extremely strong. Over the years it has gained a reputation for making unprovoked attacks and for not responding when ordered to stop. As a result, it has been outlawed in some communities.

English bulldogs still have a reputation for toughness—despite an appearance that many people find cute and endearing.

Herding Dogs

The breeds known as herding dogs were developed to guard and control sheep, cattle, and goats. Today some breeds of herding dogs are popular family pets.

The collie is probably the most popular of all herding dogs. One variety has a smooth, short-haired coat. The most common collie, however, has a rough, long-haired coat.

One of the more unusual breeds of herding dogs is the puli. Pulis are usually black in color, with a soft, thick undercoat and a long, curly outer coat. These two coats sometimes tangle together.

Other herding dogs include Australian cattle dogs, old English sheepdogs, Briards, Shetland sheepdogs, Welsh corgis, and the ever popular German shepherd. Almost all of these are now used as pets.

Herding dogs—like this Shetland sheepdog—often make excellent pets.

Dog-Shopping Decisions

If you are considering a dog as a pet, make sure to think about the time it takes to properly care for that animal. Dogs need daily attention, including walks, feeding, and grooming. They also need veterinary care. And since most dogs live a long lifespan, an owner must be willing to care for a dog for its entire life.

It is important that dog owners choose the kind of dog that is right for them. Dog breeds vary in their temperaments, or personalities. Some breeds can be more excitable, noisier, or more patient with children than others. Others are quiet and do not like to be disturbed by noisy, playing youngsters. In general, a dog and its owner should have similar temperaments.

Living space is another important factor to consider when thinking about which kind of dog to have. Large dogs require a lot of space in which to live and play. Smaller dogs, of course, need less space. As a rule, people who live in small apartments should look for dogs that weigh less than twenty-five pounds.

People choose particular dogs for many different reasons, including personal appeal.

Being a Responsible Dog Owner

When it comes to their dog's behavior, dog owners should also be considerate of other people. Some courtesies are basic.

There are "leash laws" in many communities. Responsible owners keep their dogs on leashes when walking them in public places. Leashing a dog prevents it from running into the street or possibly biting people.

Some communities have "pooper scooper" laws requiring owners to clean up their dogs' droppings on the street. Droppings should never be left on the sidewalk or on someone else's property.

Owners also should make sure that their dogs do not disturb other people with loud barking or howling. Dogs that are well trained and exercised usually do not make much unnecessary noise.

It is also important to prevent unwanted puppies that could become strays. Veterinarians can perform simple procedures called spaying and neutering that will make it impossible for female dogs to become pregnant or male dogs to father puppies.

Responsible owners obey all dog laws, including leash laws.

A New Puppy

Young dogs are called puppies. Born blind and deaf, newborns depend entirely on their mothers for food and care. Gradually their eyes and ears open, and they begin to walk. At three weeks of age puppies begin to bark and wag their tails and can start to eat solid food. Up to four months of age they need daily supplementary feedings.

The best time to get a puppy is when it is between six and eight weeks old. By this time puppies are eating on their own, and they are old enough to bond with humans.

Owners should properly prepare for having a new puppy in their house. Food dishes, toys, a collar and leash, and a bed should be purchased before bringing the puppy home.

When selecting a puppy, pet owners should check to make sure the pup is healthy. Things to look for include bright eyes, clean ears, sweet breath, and a shiny coat. The puppy should also be active and alert to its surroundings.

Puppies have a lot of energy, but they also need a lot of rest and sleep.

Housebreaking a Puppy

Sometimes the hardest part of having a new puppy is housebreaking it. Housetraining should begin as soon as a new puppy comes into your home. Depending on the breed, it could take up to twelve weeks to fully housetrain a dog. However, it is important to have reasonable expectations about housebreaking. Dogs under six months of age sometimes do not have the physical self-control to become fully trained.

A good way to begin training is to confine the puppy in a small area of the house at night and when it is left alone in the house. The area should be just big enough to hold the puppy's bed. This way the dog will wait as long as possible to urinate or move its bowels. Even puppies do not want to soil their own beds!

Dog owners must also take their pets out for walks during the day. Dogs should be walked the first thing in the morning, after waking from a nap, and about 20 minutes after each meal. A final night-time walk is also a good idea.

Training a dog takes a lot of time and personal attention.

Dog and Puppy Chow

Choosing the right food is important for the health of a dog. Breeds vary in their nutritional needs. A Great Dane puppy, for example, may develop rickets on a terrier pup's diet. Owners should consult with a pet expert to find out just what their pet needs in terms of food and vitamins.

Dogs also need different kinds of food at different stages of their lives. Puppies should eat only store-bought foods that are labeled for puppies. Usually these are balanced, high-energy dry foods.

Up to the age of three months puppies usually need to eat four times a day. The number of feedings can drop down to two meals a day when the puppy reaches six months of age.

Puppies, however, sometimes are too distracted to eat in a new home. They may need encouragement in order to keep on the proper feeding schedule. By the time they are adults, dogs usually need only one main meal a day—with the occasional treat thrown in.

Should a dog be fed table scraps under the dinner table? In general, this practice should be avoided. Inappropriate foods—veal, pork, or spicy foods—may upset the dog's stomach. It also mistakenly teaches the dog to beg!

The right foods can help keep a dog healthy and happy.

Look Who's in the Doghouse!

Some dogs really have it made! A pampered pet might have an air-conditioned doghouse and bed with a mattress and sheets. What more could a dog want? A better question is, "What does a dog really need to get its proper rest?"

A good dog bed can be as simple as a cardboard box with shredded paper and some towels. But whatever is used for bedding should be replaced or washed often. This will keep the dog clean and free of fleas. If a dog owner does a lot of traveling, a shipping crate or kennel can be used as a dog bed to help the pet become used to being in an enclosed space.

Dogs that are kept outside should be protected from the weather. A doghouse should shelter the dog from both heat and cold. The floor of the doghouse should be off the ground so that the floor does not stay damp. In severe weather, when even a good doghouse may not provide proper shelter, dogs should be brought indoors.

Sometimes a dog gets so tired that it will sleep anywhere!

Brushing a dog's coat helps keep it neat and clean.

Grooming

Grooming a dog involves much more than just combing its coat. It also means caring for a dog's teeth, nails, and ears. How often and how much time this takes depends on the breed, the condition of the dog, its size, and its coat.

Brushing a dog's coat several times a week will keep most dogs neat and clean. If a dog spends most of its time outdoors, brushing should be done more often. A bristle brush works well for dogs with any kind of coat.

Dogs need to be washed as often as necessary. Some dogs might even need a bath every week. When bathing a dog, it is important to use the right kind of shampoo. A dry shampoo, for example, is probably best for some dogs because it removes the excess oil from the dog's coat.

Dogs can develop tooth problems just like humans. So owners should brush their dog's teeth once or twice a week. To help scrape tartar off their teeth, dogs should be given hard things to chew such as canine biscuits or quality rawhide.

Visiting the Vet

As you probably know, the term "vet" is a short version of the word veterinarian, the term we use for an animal doctor.

Newly acquired dogs should be checked by a vet for any health problems. All dogs, especially puppies, should get regular checkups. Dogs need vaccinations for protection from most common dog diseases, including rabies, canine distemper, and hepatitis.

How do you know when a dog is sick? Most often a sick dog will show a change in eating habits or behavior. A sick dog may become less active. It also may eat less or even refuse to eat at all. On the other hand, with some illnesses a dog may actually want to eat more.

One of the most dangerous diseases that can strike a dog is rabies. This disease, which affects the nervous system, is fatal. It is caused by a virus and is transmitted through the bite of another infected animal. In dogs symptoms include excess salivating and seizures. Dogs with rabies may bite and infect humans.

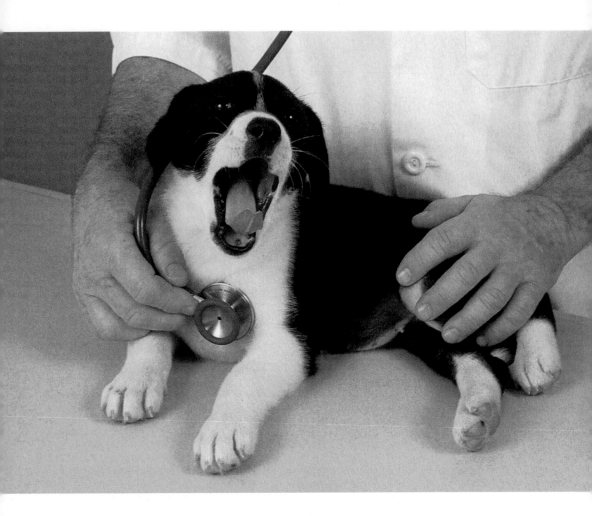

Dogs need regular checkups from a vet.

Basic Training

Puppies are a lot like babies. They will do anything to get attention. They also need guidance and direction. From the beginning owners should praise their dogs when they do something right and correct them when they do something wrong.

Every dog needs to learn at least five basic commands: sit, heel, down, stay, and come. Dogs that do not learn and obey at least these commands may never really be trusted to stay controlled in public.

Another area for training is walking. Sometimes people say that a particular dog is taking its owner for a walk. The truth is, it always should be the other way around! Dogs that pull on their leashes and drag their owners all over are not well trained.

A stern command from its owner will usually make a dog stop what it is doing. This is especially important when dogs jump—even in a friendly fashion—on people or other animals. But use of positive reinforcement is a good way to train dogs. Dog treats, petting, and words of praise are positive means of motivating dogs to please their owners.

Dog Antics

If you take some time and just watch dogs, you will probably end up laughing at some of the funny things they do!

Do you ever wonder, for example, why dogs do such silly things as chase their tails? When dogs chase their tails, they are actually playing. A puppy will naturally chase its tail because it does not think the tail is part of its body. To a puppy the tail looks like prey or something to eat! Adult dogs sometimes chase their tails because they are bored! It can be a sign that they are not getting enough attention or exercise.

Eating grass is another strange dog behavior. In general, dogs eat grass when they have stomachaches. Grass makes them vomit, which can help them feel better.

Some dogs, especially terriers, love to dig holes. Why? Well, it's just something that dogs have always done. Dogs have been digging holes for thousands of years.

Dog Shows

Many dog owners enjoy showing their dogs in dog shows and similar competitions. At these events judges evaluate dogs on their physical appearance, temperament, and movements.

In the United States the American Kennel Club (AKC) oversees most purebred dog competitions. Founded in 1884, the AKC holds more than eight thousand competitions annually.

There are three kinds of dog competitions: dog shows, field trials, and obedience trials. In a dog show judges evaluate dogs based on how well they represent their breed in appearance and present a "best of show" award to the winner.

Field trials are designed to imitate the conditions of actual hunting. Hunting dogs compete in field trials by showing how well they can locate or retrieve prey.

Obedience trials judge dogs on their performance of certain tasks. The dogs are given a series of verbal commands or hand signals, and they must respond to them correctly.

At obedience trials dogs compete to see which follows commands best.

Dog Years

Have you heard that one dog year equals seven human years? This is not necessarily true. Because dogs grow and mature at different rates, it is difficult to compare their ages to those of humans. Dogs are considered mature, or fully grown, at two years of age.

In general, smaller breeds of dogs live longer than larger breeds. A toy poodle or pug may live as long as 15 or 16 years. A Great Dane may only live eight or nine years. It is an Australian sheepdog, however, that has the longest recorded life for a dog—twenty-nine years and five months!

Quality of life is just as important as length of life. For puppies to grow up to be healthy, active, and strong adult dogs, they need loving care and attention, a healthy diet, regular exercise, and good medical care.

Small dogs like this pug can live as long as 15 or 16 years.

Lights, Camera, Action!

As long as people have enjoyed going to movies and watching television, there have been dog actors. These talented canines have provided many hours of entertainment for people.

Lassie, Benji, and Beethoven are three famous film dogs. Lassie was a fictional collie who first appeared in books, then movies, and finally television. For several generations young people—and adults as well—have been thrilled by the adventures of this amazingly clever and loyal dog.

More recently Benji was featured in a series of four movies beginning in 1974 and continuing until 1987. Beethoven, a very large and messy Saint Bernard, starred in two movies in the early 1990s. In 1996 Disney released *101 Dalmatians*, another movie that touched on people's endless affection for dogs.

Starring in movies or TV is hard work for dogs. They have special trainers and handlers to work with them. Often several dogs that look alike will perform different scenes on film.

Words to Know

American Kennel Club (AKC)   The organization that supervises dog shows and registers dog breeds in the United States.

Canine   Another word for dog.

Domestic   Tame or adapted to living with humans.

Flush   To chase prey from hiding places.

Instincts   An animal's natural, inherited abilities.

Mature   Fully grown.

Mongrel   A mixed-breed dog or a dog of unknown parents.

Muzzle   The projecting nose and jaws of a dog.

Neuter   To operate on a male dog so that he cannot reproduce.

Point   To stop and wait in a particular position.

Prey   An animal hunted by another animal.

Purebred   A dog whose parents are a recognized breed.

Rabies   A fatal disease that causes dogs to become irritable and bite.

Spay   To operate on a female dog so that she cannot reproduce.

Trait   An inherited characteristic.

Vaccinate   To inject, or give a shot to, an animal to prevent disease.

Veterinarian   A doctor who takes care of animals.

INDEX

Cover Photo: Karen Helsinger Mullen (Unicorn Stock Photos)
Photo Credits: Norvia Behling (Behling & Johnson Photography), pages 11, 17, 20, 23, 25, 29, 31, 33, 35, 36, 39, 43; Shirley Haley (Top Shots), page 8; Ed Harp (Unicorn Stock Photos), page 26; Karen Helsinger Mullen (Unicorn Stock Photos), page 7; SuperStock, Inc., pages 13, 14, 45; Aneal Vohra (Unicorn Stock Photos), page 4.